LEADER'S
EDITION

I Thought You Were My Friend!

KAREN ▼ DOCKREY

Student books
are available for use
in group study.

VICTOR BOOKS

A DIVISION OF SCRIPTURE PRESS PUBLICATIONS INC.
USA CANADA ENGLAND

ABOUT THE AUTHOR

Karen Dockrey has worked with teens and their leaders for over 20 years. She served two churches as minister of youth and currently spends her professional time writing for youth and their leaders. Her 22 books include *The Youth Worker's Guide to Creative Bible Study* (Victor) and two other Life Support Small Group studies: *What's a Kid Like Me Doing in a Family Like This?* and *Are You There, God?* She earned a Master of Divinity degree from Southern Baptist Theological Seminary and currently works with youth at Bluegrass Baptist Church in Hendersonville, Tennessee.

Cover Design: Grace Chan Mallette
ISBN: 1-56476-281-5

1 2 3 4 5 6 7 8 9 10   Printing/Year   98   97   96   95   94

Produced for Victor Books by the Livingstone Corporation. David Veerman and Michael Kendrick, project staff.

CONTENTS

INTRODUCTION

Small Group Studies

Friendship is a skill and like all skills it grows with training and practice. This small group study is designed to provide this skill training and practice. Small group studies are designed to create an environment for your members that will (1) provide acceptance for them just as they are, (2) challenge them with God's truth to be who He calls them to be, and (3) offer a supportive community to strengthen their personal and spiritual growth. Within the context of meaningful, interpersonal relationships, each session seeks the healing and wholeness of persons through their personal encounters with the grace and holiness of Jesus Christ. Just as the community grew together in Acts 2, as the body served together in 1 Corinthians 12, and the church was equipped together in Ephesians 4, so will your group experience the reality that in Christ we become more than just the sum of our individual members when we meet together, just as we are, to become just who He calls us to be.

Contemporary culture, specifically that of adolescents, offers very little opportunity for interpersonal intimacy. Students need a safe place for healing and a supportive place for growth into wholeness. They need a place to go where they can take off the masks they use to cover insecurities and uncertainty about who they are as persons. They are also searching for a place where they can find meaning through making a contribution to the lives of others. Your students require the security of belonging to a significant community of peers in order to develop their own identities in Christ. Small group studies enable you to meet these needs for individuals who are at all levels of personal and spiritual maturity. The only prerequisite for being a member of these small groups is a heart willing to develop relationships with friends. The potential for growth is as limitless as the potential for God's work in your individual and corporate lives.

SESSION OVERVIEW

Each session begins with a summary of the small group experience which has been prepared for your group.

Purpose states the intent of the session, clearly defining the overall thrust of this particular small group experience.

Needs briefly examines the needs of group members in relation to the topic and Scripture. Attention will also be given to group issues.

Goals lists objectives by which you can (1) adapt the material specifically for your small group (2) evaluate the effectiveness of the session in measurable terms.

Life Response suggests a commitment each group member can make to live out the lesson during the week. Additional suggestions for groups with higher commitment levels follow each session.

Resource Materials outlines what you will need in order to lead the group through each session.

HEARTBEAT

These opening exercises and experiences are designed to take a pulse, to get to the heart of who students are. They focus group members on the question, **"What kind of friend am I?"** Active listening and accurate affirmation are the key ingredients in this first step toward community building.

LIFELINE

Discovery of God's Word is the dynamic element in these active Bible studies. The personal, practical exploration of **"What kind of friend does God call me to be?"** is the focus of the group's interaction with biblical truth. As group members deepen in their knowledge and broaden in their understanding of Jesus Christ's lordship, they will move toward relevant application of this truth in their own personal context.

BODYLIFE

Your group members will experience the reality of the love of the Body as they commit themselves corporately to being all of who God calls them to be. Personal ownership of the truth discovered in LIFELINE enables students to make new commitments toward God-centered friendships. Through affirmation, prayer, and encouragement, they will realize that the love in Christian peer support is greater than the fear of the world's peer pressure.

HINTS & HELPS

☞ **HELPS:** sensitize you to student concerns and questions which may arise in response to the topic or structure of the session. These insights and resources will help you prepare for the challenges of leading a small group through the community experience of being who God calls them to be.

☞ **HINTS:** develop small group leadership skills. These technical points of advice will support you in your challenging role.

GROUP MEMBER AND LEADER MATERIALS

Group members' workbooks include the main content of the HEARTBEAT, LIFELINE, and BODYLIFE sections of each session. All of the group member's material is reproduced in this leader's edition. Additional exercises and activities in the leader's edition are printed in **boldface**. These additional resources allow you maximum flexibility for working with your group.

PREPARATION

To prepare, become familiar with the purposes, needs, and goals of each session. Then adapt the session content for your group. Some groups may need added emphasis on the HEARTBEAT section. Other groups, either because of group members' personal maturity or depth of relationships, will have a community foundation which will enable them to focus more time in the LIFELINE and BODYLIFE sections. In either case, meet students at their points of need.

Group members will not need to prepare in advance for the sessions. As the LIFELINE and BODYLIFE impact lives, however, student commitments establish the need for follow-through and loving, community accountability. This accountability can be naturally incorporated into the following session's heartbeat section.

Prayer is the ultimate source of preparation for both you and your group. The materials provided for you will encourage and support your efforts to integrate prayer into every phase of this small group series.

Look Past the Myths to Build True Friendship

SESSION OVERVIEW

Purpose:
This session guides group members to define friendship in true and godly ways, ways that bring the closeness they long for.

Needs:
Adolescents wonder why their friendships don't match certain expectations. These expectations may come from fairy tales, television, books, or from watching others. Sadly, each of these sources tend to show the benefits of friendship without displaying its struggles and problems. So, adolescents live in loneliness because they believe certain myths about friendships. But as adolescents see friendship as it really is, they find freedom to build lasting relationships.

Adolescents tend to assume that others don't like or need them. So they wait for friends to come to them. The truth is, others are also waiting. By making the first move, a young person can begin to build happy friendships. They can bring companionship to someone lonely, joy to someone sad, truth to someone who believes lies.

Adolescents glorify or deny God through the way they relate to others. Encourage and equip them to glorify God through their friendships.

Goals:

The goals for the *leader* include

(1) guiding group members to recognize why they value friendship;

(2) pointing members to biblical principles that lead to closeness;

(3) challenging members to commit to grow their friend-ships.

The goals for the *group members* are that they will

(1) describe why friendship matters to them;

(2) replace friendship myths with truths;

(3) take steps to keep their friendships "in step with the Spirit" (Gal. 5:25).

Life Response:

Group members will commit to actions that begin and grow friendships.

Resource Materials:

___ Bibles

___ pens or pencils

___ one copy of *I Thought You Were My Friend!* for each member

___ 3 X 5 index cards (24 per pair or quartet of group members)

 **HEARTBEAT**

As group members enter, have them to choose an item in the room that reminds them of friendship. Then have them complete this activity.

Notice Why You Value Friends

Create your own object lesson by choosing an item on you (your clothes or accessories), with you (in your billfold or purse), or around you (in the room) and telling how it is like and unlike friendship:

Friendship is like this _____________ because . . .

But friendship is different from this _______________ because . . .

As others in the group share their object lessons, jot down words that describe friendship:

☞ **[HELP: Sample words include: togetherness; trust; truth; understanding; fun; life-sharing; company; cozy; talking; listening; helping; caring; equipping, supporting]**

Grow More Mature Relationships

You may have noticed by now that your friendships differ from the kind you had as a small child. Then, friends were the boys and girls who played with you and attended your birthday parties. Your parents may have done much to arrange those times with your friends. Now your friendships include not only play, but learning, life choices, advice-giving, support, encouragement, and more. Your friendships are more your responsibility. You make the phone calls and arrange to get together. You choose who you will spend time with and why. This makes friendship more complicated, but also more precious.

Why are friendships important to you now? Choose your favorite reason from the list below or write your own. Then talk to the group for about 30 seconds on your choice. Begin with "This friendship factor is important because . . ."

_________ *Friends help me know myself better.* My friends can help me be who I am and who God has made me to be.

_________ *Friends draw me toward God.* Good friends can give me the motivation and confidence to obey, love, and honor God.

_________ *Friends help mold my character.* My friends can bring out the honesty, trust, caring, and skill in me. I can do the same for them.

_________ *Friendships form a bridge between the family I was born into and the family I will someday belong to.* I'll choose a mate from my friends. Also, my friends will be like family when I'm away from home.

_________ *Friendships help my relationships with family and fellow workers.* We can help each other get along with people.

_________ *Friends are fun to be with.* I like sharing play, work, school, service, problems, spiritual growth, all of life with my friends.

Describe the actions and attitudes of a friend who does or could do one of the above for you:

How will you do the above for the people you encounter?

☞ **[HELP: The 30-second speeches enable students to express convictions and teach each other. Use students' words to bring out details like:**

• *Friends help me know myself better.* Choose to grow closest to friends who see and encourage God's best in you, who bring out your strengths rather than stifle them. Equally important, choose friends who see your weaknesses and help you replace them with God's strength. Let your friends help you learn who

you are and how to daily demonstrate your faith.

• *Friends draw each other toward or away from God.* Friends can give an accurate or twisted view of God with their words and actions. They can encourage obedience or disobedience, partnership with God or rebellion against Him, friendship with God or alienation from Him. It is more possible to relate healthily to the real God when we have friends who understand and live for God. Hebrews 10:24-25 summarizes this principle.

• *Friends help mold character development.* Very simply, we become like the people we spend time with. Though family plays the strongest role, friends mold values, priorities, choices, and levels of obedience to God. We want some friends who are nonbelievers or nonpracticing believers so we can draw them to Jesus, but our closest friendships should be with fellow believers who obey God in daily life (2 Cor. 6:14).

• *Friendships form a bridge between the family of birth and the family we will form later.* As we grow we spend more time with friends. Often we room with a friend after high school and choose a mate from our friends. Our parents were once friends who became family. Choose friends who can be like family.

• *Friendships help relationships with family and fellow workers.* With friends we learn to solve or avoid problems, cooperate or compete, show compassion or explain away pain, express or quench feelings, build each other up or tear each other down, serve or take advantage of. These crucial relationship skills form the basis for happiness or misery. Choose friends who encourage the best qualities in you.

• *Friends are fun to be with.* Good friendships are simply enjoyable. Life's pleasures are better when shared with a friend. Life's disasters are more bearable when a friend goes through them with us. Companionship is one of God's finest gifts. The best marriages and working relationships are based in friendship.]

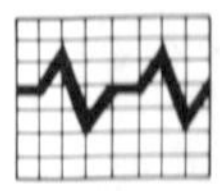 **LIFELINE**

Debunk Friendship Myths

You may have noticed also that your friendships are different than you expected them to be. You expected true friends to be always easy to get along with, continually caring, and available at all times. But sometimes your friends are a burden rather than being fun. Sometimes your friends are self-centered rather than caring. Sometimes your friends are busy and are not available to you. When these problems happen constantly, your friendship may be in danger. But when these conflicts happen occasionally, you will recognize that they are part of the bittersweet process of getting along with another human being. Real-life friendships are formed by imperfect people who won't always act as they should or could.

Rather than let this discourage you, let it prompt you to act. Work with your friends to move your friendships toward greater good. If a friend is unwilling to do this, spend less time with this friend and move to others.

Begin deeper quality in your friendships by finding the truth about friendship and living it. When you believe a myth about friendship, you could end up letting yourself and others down. For example, if you believe strong friendships just happen, you won't know that you must put effort into friendship. If you think true friends never hurt each other, you'll assume you can never make up with a friend who made a mistake. You'll lose rather than gain friends.

What's dangerous about each of the following friendship myths? Match each myth with one of the stories listed below. Then notice how living biblical truth found in Galatians 5:13-26 would improve friendship.

☞ **[HINT: As they work, ask group members: Why is the way in Galatians 5:13-26 a better way to build friendships? What other Bible passages show the danger of these myths and the better way of the truth?]**

_______ MYTH #1. The best friendships just happen.
_______ MYTH #2. A true friend will never hurt you.
_______ MYTH #3. True friends never disagree.
_______ MYTH #4. A friend will do whatever the other asks.
_______ MYTH #5. True friends just overlook the bad.
_______ MYTH #6. Strong friendships come easily.

☞ **[HELP: The correct matches are 1-C; 2-A; 3-F; 4-E; 5-B; 6-D.]**

A. Terry began ignoring Jan to spend more and more time with popular people. Terry didn't mean to hurt Jan. Terry just let his desire for acceptance crowd out their friendship. What Terry didn't realize was that maintaining a close friendship with Jan would have made him more secure and happy. Terry took Jan for granted rather than valuing Jan for the fascinating friend he is.

Terry, like all people, is an imperfect human trying to learn what to do and how to do it. In the process Terry will make some wise and some foolish choices. Terry's choice to value popularity more than genuineness was foolish. It hurt Jan. But it doesn't have to be the end of their friendship. Terry and Jan can choose to talk about the things that hurt them, ask and seek forgiveness, and move on to do good for each other.

Galatians 5:25-26 suggests that even Christians still struggle with doing right. To move on, Terry must see the value of a true friendship, and Jan must be willing to forgive. Then both must show active and steady care for each other. How have or could you move on after a friendship fight? What made this hard? Easy?

B. Kim is critical and bossy. When friends ask Kim to change, Kim simply explains that this is the way she is. She doesn't mean to be bossy; she's just always been that way and can't help it.

As Galatians 5:16-18 illustrates, Kim suffers from letting her sinful nature rule. Even though she is a Christian, she thinks nothing of letting her selfish attitudes reign. Rather than let the Holy Spirit cleanse her life, she expects her friends to excuse her behavior. *After all,* she thinks, *that's the way I am.* Kim claims that she can't help her behavior—but the problem is not that she can't, but that she won't. Though it's true that friends accept each other, warts and all, Kim's friends do her a disservice by tolerating her cruel behavior. True friends would encourage her to change by telling her how her behavior hurts them. They might refuse to spend time with Kim when she acts bossy or whiny. How or when have you motivated a friend to make a change for the better?

C. Stacy waited for friends to come to him. He assumed that if no one talked to him, no one liked him. He complained that everybody at his school was snobby and that he didn't fit in. In truth, the others were shy and hoping he would talk to them. Or they had tried speaking, but Stacy did not respond.

The best friendships happen as a result of deliberate caring efforts like saying hello, listening, inviting acquaintances to go places, and sharing ideas, feelings, and dreams. As Ryan began to do these things, he found friends. He discovered, as explained in Galatians 5:13-15, that his freedom as a Christian allowed him to indulge himself and wait for another person to initiate a friendship. But this choice didn't bring fulfillment or friendship. His complainy talk brought no closeness either. Finally, he chose to serve and love as he wanted to be served and loved. As he showed friendship, he found the friends he'd been seeking. How has this happened to you?

D. Sam was shocked at how hard it was to live with Nat. They had been friends all through high school, but living in the same dorm room at college was a disaster. Sam stayed up late, but Nat went to bed early. Nat liked to study with music on, but Sam liked it quiet. The two were surprised by these sudden disagreements. They had been certain that they would get along better than roommates ever had.

Any two people will have disagreements and rough spots, especially when they live together or spend lots of time together. It's part of being human. It's part of close friendship. The actions in Galatians 5:13-26 are seldom easy, but friendship makes them worth it. Sam can use gentleness when moving around the room while Nat is asleep (v. 23). Nat can use kindness by wearing earphones to hear his study music (v. 22). Each can serve the other rather than biting and devouring the other (vv. 13-15). As they do these things, their friendship will grow instead of deteriorate. Knowing friendship can be hard makes us more aware of what we have to do to keep it strong. Sam and Nat started acting out of love for each other even when they didn't feel like it. When have you willed yourself to start acting differently for the sake of someone else, even though it wasn't convenient for you?

E. Kelly tried to persuade Frank to let him look at his paper during the test. Kelly said a true friend would help. After all, the reason Kelly hadn't studied more was that he had been at church the night before. Frank said he was a true friend but couldn't help Kelly do something dishonest.

Friends will do what is right, not what is requested. A true friend will help his friend do well, choose well, care well, and be honest. Galatians 5:19-21 describes some actions a friend won't do for anyone, especially another friend. Which of these have friends asked you to do? How do you do what is right and maintain your friendship?

F. Chris was shocked the first time Lesley disagreed with her. Didn't true friends agree on everything? How could Lesley say Chris's view on sports was wrong? As a friend, shouldn't Lesley support what Chris said?

One of the lovely things about humans is their diversity. We are different and can learn from each other. The disagreement Chris and Lesley had was a simple difference of opinion, helpful and necessary to a friendship. As Galatians 5:15 and 26 explain, Chris and Lesley can disagree on such matters without provoking and envying. How have you learned from disagreeing with a friend who had a different opinion than you?

But there is a disagreement that is dangerous to both friendships and people: disagreement about the truth. Friends cannot disagree over the basics spelled out in Galatians 5:19-23. The actions listed in vv. 19-20 are wrong and the actions described in vv. 22-23 are right, no matter what we think about them. How have you helped a friend see and live the truth? How has a friend done this for you?

Now choose one myth and explain with an example from your own life why living by that myth would be dangerous to a friendship. How will you live truth instead?

☞ **[HINT: As group members report, assign each a myth, encourage them to read aloud the related verses from Galatians, and invite an explanation from experience. After all have reported, guide each to summarize friend-**

ship truths by choosing two and explaining how they work together. Examples:

• A friendship based in truth doesn't JUST HAPPEN. Friendships begin as two people make a point to talk to each other. It takes deliberate attention and communication to know what a friend feels and needs. This effort produces a togetherness that keeps you from HURTing friends.

• A good friend won't DO WHATEVER THE OTHER asks when that request is one of the sinful actions described in Galatians 5:19-20. Instead of just OVER-LOOKING THE BAD, a friend will help the other to do right.

• When friends DISAGREE, they can talk without biting and devouring each other (vv. 13-15). This does not COME EASILY but the results are good.]

Take Action

Choose people who like you, enjoy life, and show their dedication to God in the way they treat people. Then, rather than wait for them to come to you, act. Use friendship-building actions like those found in Galatians 5:13-15, 22-26.

Together with a partner, create a Slap Stack that will help you memorize actions that hurt or help friendships. Find these characteristics in Galatians 5:19-23. Write one characteristic on each index card until all have been recorded. Shuffle the cards and divide them evenly between you and your partner. Display them face down. Take turns flipping a card and try to be the first to slap the helpful-to-friendship actions (listed in verses 22-23). When you slap the card, tell why the action would help by citing an example from a friendship you know. If time allows, play the game again, this time slapping the harmful-to-friendship actions and citing examples of how each characteristic hurts friendships.

☞ **[HELP: Group members might say *joy* helps friendships because someone who is already happy makes a steadier friend than one who clings to a friend for joy. They might say *selfish* ambition hurts friendships because wanting a status or privilege can make one betray a friend.]**

☞ **[HINT: Allow pairs or quartets to make and play this game during the session. Writing each action on a card and playing the game helps them memorize the friendship actions. The ones to slap: love, joy, peace, patience, kindness, goodness, faithfulness, gentleness, self-control.]**

After you play, check your learning by circling the helpful-to-friendship actions and crossing out the harmful-to-friendship actions:

debauchery	discord	dissensions
drunkenness	envy	factions
faithfulness	fits of rage	gentleness
goodness	hatred	idolatry
impurity	jealousy	joy
kindness	love	orgies
patience	peace	self-control
selfish ambition	sexual immorality	witchcraft

1. The helpful characteristic I most need right now in my friendships is _________ because . . .

2. The harmful friendship action I most need to omit from my friendships right now is _________ because . . .

BODYLIFE

Keep in Step with the Spirit

Galatians 5:25 encourages us to "keep in step" with the Spirit of God. How would you explain this phrase and why?

☐ Walk in the steps God takes right in front of you (like when a child follows in her parent's footprints to make her way in the snow).
☐ Keep the same tempo, rhythm, and mood God uses to care for people.
☐ Let your words and actions be guided by God.
☐ Other: ....

1. How can you tell if a friend or potential friend is "in step with the Spirit"?

2. How can you make sure you are "in step with the Spirit" in the way you treat friends?

Life Response

In these three footprints, write the steps you think God wants you to take next in your friendships to "keep in step with the Spirit" (v. 25). Use at least one word from Galatians 5:13-26 in each action:

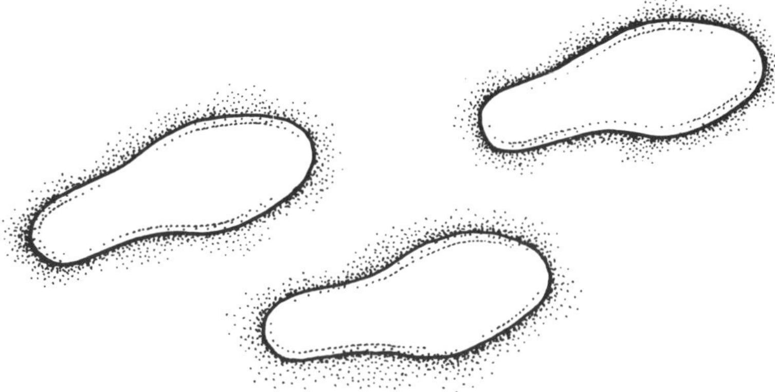

☞ **[HELP: Additional Life Responses to include if time allows or to suggest for home follow-through:**

1. Write a recipe for true friendship. What are the ingredients? How much of each ingredient is needed?

How should these ingredients be combined or prepared? How do you bake the ingredients so the friendship comes out the way you had hoped?

2. Keep a friendship journal in which you write letters to God, telling Him your thoughts about and experiences with friends. Invite God to steer your words and actions in a direction that builds friendship.]

What's Next?

What do you do when problems come? How well do you let problems lead to deeper understanding and true togetherness?

Solve Your Friendship Problems

SESSION OVERVIEW

Purpose:

Even the best friendships have problems occasionally. This session focuses on actions, words, and attitudes that can solve or prevent those problems.

Needs:

Adolescents do one of two things when they face a friendship problem: they assume it's their fault or they blame their friend. It is better to view the problem as something they both have likely contributed to. When friends recognize that conflicts happen even in the best relationships, they can stop placing blame. They can attack the problem rather than each other.

If a problem bothers either partner in a friendship, it's important enough to address. This session explores how to bring up a problem, what attitudes and words to use while solving it, and how to leave the problem behind to get on with the joy of friendship. It also affirms the difficulty of problem solving. When adolescents know that resolving conflict is supposed to be hard, they can put their energy into solving the problem without becoming discouraged.

When problems come, adolescents wonder whether to continue the friendship. The strongest friends are those who solve their disagreements, not those who avoid them. Some problems signal danger, however: indifference to God; physical or emotional abuse; substance abuse; lying through actions or words; friendships that remain one-sided. This session cautions group members against continuing such friendships, suggesting that instead they pray faithfully for person who shows the bad behavior.

Goals:

The goals for the *leader* include

(1) guiding group members to notice ways they respond to problems;

(2) equipping members with specific problem-solving actions and attitudes;

(3) facilitating the practice of problem solving.

The goals for the *group members* are that they will

(1) recognize how to match a loving response to a particular problem;

(2) notice why Jesus' advice works better than typical worldly responses;

(3) specify a "weedish" behavior to omit so they can grow loving friendships.

Life Response:

Group members will embrace actions, attitudes, and words that will solve friendship problems.

Resource Materials:

___ Bibles

___ pens or pencils

___ one copy of *I Thought You Were My Friend!* for each member

___ posters or drawings of road signs (see HEARTBEAT)

 **HEARTBEAT**

Create life-size posters of the road signs listed below and display them in the room. As group members enter, direct each to stand by the sign that best describes how they react when a problem comes. All signs must be chosen before any person is allowed to choose one that someone has selected previously. Direct them to complete this section and share their responses from the road sign location in the room.

Watch for Road Signs

Last time we described great friendships and pinpointed ways to grow them. But even the strongest friendships have problems from time to time. And not all friendships are strong. Name three problems you have had, or could have, in a friendship:

______________   ______________   ______________

Next, circle the road sign that tells what you typically do when problems occur in your friendships:

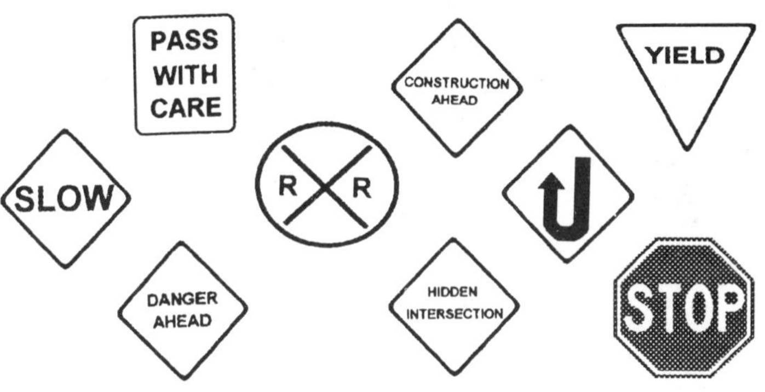

Why do you choose that action? ______________________

Did you know that each road sign indicates an action that can be the right choice, depending on the kind of problem? Under each sign, write a circumstance that would invite the response indicated by the road sign.

☞ **[HELP: Stress that the nature of the problem and the way you do the "road sign" action determines the effectiveness of the solution. Guide group members standing by each sign to give examples of how that action can help solve a problem. Possibilities: YIELD when you have been stubbornly holding back; STOP when you're about to attack your friend; wait for the RAILROAD to clear of defensiveness before you start talking about a problem; watch for HIDDEN problems rather than assume you know what's wrong; take SHARP CURVES slowly by listening before reacting; be SLOW to get angry and fast to affirm how important the friend is; watch for DANGER like a friend who lies to you; see mutual solutions as a way to CONSTRUCT closer friendships; carefully PASS obstacles to get your friendship where it should be.]**

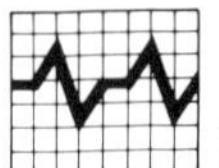 **LIFELINE**

Attack the Problem Together

Jesus gave advice on solving problems between believers in passages like Matthew 18:15-17. Inserted into this re-telling are methods people tend to use instead. Find the faulty advice and replace it with Jesus' advice — the advice that works. Work in pairs; one of you read Matthew 18:15-17 aloud while the other corrects the bogus retelling:

If your brother sins against you, wait for him to come to

____

you, and just be sure everyone knows what he has done. If

____

he listens to you, emphasize that you were right. But if he

____

will not listen, find a way to get back at him. If he refuses

____

to listen to you, then all hope is lost. And if he refuses to

listen even to the church, refuse to speak to him again.

☞ **[HELP: The corrections: *wait for him to come to you should be* "go and show him his fault"; *just be sure everyone knows what he has done* should be "just between the two of you"; *emphasize that you were right* should be "you have won your brother over"; *find a way to get back at him* should be "take one or two others along so that every matter may be established by the testimony of two or three witnesses"; *to you then* should be "to them"; *all hope is lost* should be "tell it to the church"; *refuse to ever speak to him again* should be "treat him as you would a pagan or a tax collector."]**

Jesus gave further advice for Christian friendships in verses 18-20. These actions prevent problems as well as provide ways to move on after a problem. Find a verse in Matthew 18:15-20 that answers:

_______ A. How do I bring up a problem?
_______ B. Who brings up the problem?
_______ C. What two options do I have if private talk doesn't work?
_______ D. If neither option works, what verse advises trying to win my friend to the truth similar to the way I'd win a nonbeliever to the Gospel?
_______ E. What verse suggests friends can do more together than individually?
_______ F. What verses encourage friends to pray and worship God together?

☞ **[HELP: A=v. 15; B=you do, v. 15. Explain that the one bothered by the problem is the one to bring it up.**

Friends can't "just know" what's wrong. They must talk; C = vv. 16-17. Clarify that this is asking for help, not tattling. Explain that the witnesses and church members serve as mediators, ones who help friends talk things out. Ask: Why would caring Christians be the best mediators? What's the difference between genuinely asking for help and tattling or gossiping?; D = v. 17. Stress that treating a person as a pagan or tax collector does not mean snubbing or rejecting him or her. It means lessening contact with that person while still trying to win him or her back. Ask: How do you win over a nonbeliever? E = v. 18; F = vv. 19-20.]

Choose Helpful Attitudes, Actions, and Words

It takes good attitudes, actions, and words to solve friendship problems. Find some by coming at the problem backwards. What attitudes, actions, and phrases would make a friendship problem worse? In the columns below, list at least five more problem-worsening attitudes, actions, and words.

☞　[HINT: To complete this section, divide group members into pairs. Challenge each pair to come up with problem-worsening attitudes, actions, and words. Have them do the same for problem-bettering attitudes, actions, and words. Have the teams compete to see who can come up with the most complete lists.]

Problem WORSEners

Attitudes	Actions	Words
holding a grudge	gossip	"I hate you!"
being defensive	accusing in public	"How could you?"

What is the opposite of each problem WORSEner? Let these samples help you think of more BETTERers that would solve problems rather than make them worse. List at least five of each in the columns below:

Problem BETTERers

Attitudes	**Actions**	**Words**
understand feelings	talk privately	"That really hurt me."
treat as I'd want to be treated	work together	"Can we work it out?"

God can equip us to build solid friendships. He knows the solutions to our friendship struggles and the ways to prevent future problems. The way you solve your friendship problems is a powerful way to glorify God. Why?

☞ **[HELP: Samples: Because God is interested in every area of life, everything we do can bring glory (positive attention) to Him. When we solve our problems lovingly, we take care of people, God's most precious creation. When we get along with people, others wonder why. It's a good way to give testimony to God. At the same time, when we claim to love God, but treat people badly, we hurt God, the people, and others who watch.]**

Matthew 18:15 begins with "your brother," meaning fellow believer. Why is living as an obedient believer central to solving friendship problems?

Even after you've solved a problem with a friend, you may find it hard to go on with the friendship. What makes going on hard for you?

☐ lack of trust

☐ fear the friend will hurt me again

☐ need time to heal

☐ don't want another problem to happen

☐ still angry

☐ still wonder why he/she did it

☐ ___________________________

What makes it easier for you to go on with a friendship?

☐ time

☐ knowing that all friendships have struggles

☐ recalling a time I messed up

☐ getting together with that person a little at first, more later

☐ trying to imitate God's love

☐ remembering why I liked the friend

☐ ___________________________

The strongest friends are those who solve their disagreements, not those who have none. Why?

Not all friendships should go on. Times when friends must spend less time together, be less close, or must part include:

- when one friend habitually lies or otherwise deceives the other;
- when one friend uses or abuses the other;
- when one friend uses or abuses drugs (including alcohol);
- when the relationship is one-sided because one friend is selfish;

- when one friend is indifferent to God or to obeying God.

What makes it hard for you to back off from a friendship, even one that is harmful?

☐ wanting not to seem like a snob

☐ thinking my friend might change

☐ fear that I won't find other friends

☐ fear that I'll hurt my friend

☐ not wanting to be disloyal

☐ not sure if I should or not

☐ wanting to continue the friendship even though it's not in my best interests

☐ _______________________

What danger would make you more willing to put some distance between you and a hurtful friend?

☐ friend could pull me into wrongdoing

☐ I would lose my life (from alcohol- or drug-related crash, or from physical abuse)

☐ I would suffer emotionally because my friend won't meet my needs

☐ I would suffer emotionally because I'd believe I deserve the bad treatment I was receiving

☐ Dangerous behavior would keep me from seeing myself as a valuable creation of God

☐ Continuing that friendship allows that friend to hurt others, including me

☐ Continuing a one-sided friendship feeds my friend's selfishness

☐ Continuing this friendship makes it look like I approve of the behavior

☐ _______________________

Why is prayerful support better than close friendship in abusive, one-sided, or God-ignoring friendships?

BODYLIFE

Spot the Myths

Problem solving has its own set of myths, such as *She should just know how I feel!* Why is talking crucial to solving or preventing problems?

A second myth is *A true friend will just overlook the bad. Why is this a myth? What is the truth?*

Solve the Specifics

It's much easier to know how to solve a problem than it is to actually solve one. Practice solving problems with these examples. Find at least one phrase in Matthew 18:15-20 or another favorite Bible passage to guide you and your friend as you solve problems like these.

☞ **[HINT: Try one of these variations on the "read-and-discuss" standard:**

• Have group members act out what the two friends do and say, including how to handle defensiveness, pride, and other obstacles.

• Invite group members to act and speak in ways that would make the problem worse and then in ways that would make it better. Ask: Why do we often make things worse rather than better in real life?

• Let a third person help the friends solve problems as in Matthew 18:16. Ask: When is it helpful to have a mediator? What kind of mediator might muddle things?]

A. Liu's family has lived in the United States for generations. But because he is Asian-American, people treat him as a foreigner. Why can't people see that all persons, except Native Americans, came here from a different country? Ross seems to understand this. He has always treated

Liu as a person of value. He doesn't even think about race. But yesterday Liu heard Ross laugh at a racial joke. It wasn't about Liu, but Liu felt that if Ross would laugh at that joke, he'd laugh at one about him.

1. What feelings do Liu and Ross have about this situation?

2. What Scripture sheds light on this problem? With what words and actions might God want Liu to bring up the problem?

3. With what words and actions does God want Ross to respond?

4. What attitudes does God want Liu to display? Ross?

5. What false perceptions might be contributing to this problem? (Example: Liu thinks one sin automatically leads to another; Ross thinks it's OK to laugh at jokes about people.) How might the two friends live the truth?

B. Dana struggles with the way friends perceive his faith. They have preconceived ideas about Christianity and assume certain things without ever asking. Like last week the guys were bragging about their sexual escapades and asked Dana when he was going to have sex. He said, "On my wedding night." They all laughed and Tony said, "Don't you like girls, Dana?" It's not that Dana doesn't like girls; he likes them so much that he doesn't want to use them. Dana feels lonely and misunderstood, especially by Tony. Dana's a guy with standards, not a frustrated prig who never has any fun.

1. What feelings do Dana and Tony have about this situation?

2. What Scripture sheds light on this problem? With

what words and actions might God want Dana to bring up the problem?

3. With what words and actions does God want Tony to respond?

4. What attitudes does God want Dana to display? Tony?

5. What false perceptions might be contributing to this problem? (Examples: Dana thinks nobody understands; Tony thinks a true man has sex before marriage.) How might they live the truth?

C. Kristy and Meghan had been best friends for years. This past summer Meghan noticed Kristy pulling away. Invitations to her house came less frequently. Now Kristy says less and less to Meghan, especially if anyone else is there to talk to. Kristy seems enamored with wealth and looks, and status seems more important to her than character. Meghan feels hurt, angry, and betrayed. She sees no way they can ever be close again.

1. What feelings do Kristy and Meghan have about this situation?

2. What Scripture sheds light on this problem? With what words and actions might God want Meghan to bring up the problem?

3. With what words and actions does God want Kristy to respond to it?

4. What attitudes does God want Meghan to display? Kristy?

5. What false perceptions might be contributing to this

problem? (Examples: Kristy thinks you have to be a person of looks or money to be a quality friend; Meghan thinks a problem with a friend means you can never be close again.) How might each be encouraged to live the truth?

D. Describe a friendship problem you may be having now.

1. What feelings do you and your friend have about this situation?

2. What Scripture sheds light on this problem? With what words and actions might God want you to bring up the problem?

3. With what words and actions does God want your friend to respond?

4. What attitudes does God want you to display? your friend?

5. What false perceptions might be contributing to this problem? How might you and your friend live the truth?

Life Response

Solving friendship problems is like tending a garden. Gardens need daily care to keep the weeds out and the good plants growing well. To keep your friendship healthy, you must weed out behavior that creates distance and cultivate actions that grow closeness.

Weed out the distance-creators by recognizing them, talking about them, and refusing to let them continue. Cultivate the closeness-growers by intentionally doing actions that make friendships better. In the space below, jot down a list of the "weeds" that may be affecting the growth of your friendships. What weedish behaviors do you display?

Are you argumentative? selfish? moody? demanding?

Now think of the actions God wants you to take to remove the weeds from your friendships. How will weeding prevent problems as well as solve them?

How will you cultivate the plants without encouraging weeds to grow?

When you focus on taking care of the good plants, you deliberately do right. How does deliberately doing right keep you from accidentally hurting a friend?

☞ **[HELP: Encourage group members to specify a specific weedish behavior they'll delete and a caring behavior they'll do. Suggest that students cultivate actions found in Matthew 18:15-20 and in their favorite Bible verses. Samples:**

understanding	**kind words**	**acceptance**
cooperation	**support**	**other-centeredness**
communication	**sensitivity**	**listening**
swallowed pride	**honesty**	**attention**
depending on God	**respect**	**letting others mediate**

Weeds they may want to get rid of include biting, devouring, bickering, slamming, competing, gossiping, slandering, being self-centered, and more.]

☞ **[HELP: Additional Life Responses to include if time allows or to suggest for home follow-through:**
    1. Because a good marriage is a good friendship, invite a happily married couple to talk about ways they have solved problems and created closeness over the years.
    2. Think about a friend with whom you have a rift. What action does God want you to take to solve it?

What hesitation do you have about trying to repair the relationship? What advice from Matthew 18:15-20 might work?

3. Write a series of three to five questions to ask when solving a problem between you and a friend. Let the questions form a word for easy memory. The letters from the word HELP might stand for the following questions: "*How* did I contribute to this problem?"; "How will I *explain* to my friend what bothers me?"; "Can we *list* everything we feel like doing to solve the problem and then choose the one that would help most?"; "What *prayer* will I pray for God's guidance throughout the process?"]

What's Next?
Do you talk too much or too little? Why is it easier to talk to some people than others? How can you use talking and listening to create joy?

▼

THREE

Provide Interested Listening and Caring Talk

SESSION OVERVIEW

Purpose:

This session will guide group members to embrace and practice interested listening and caring talk to build close friendships.

Needs:

The last session was on problems. Many, if not most, problems can be avoided or solved with clear communication. This session practices communication skills. Good communication is not only preventive and restorative; it's fun. When friends communicate well and understand each other clearly, they find joy in being together and joy in sharing life.

Adolescents wonder what makes it easier to talk to some people than to others. They wonder why some people seem to find it easy to talk to everyone. This session affirms that listening and talking are skills that improve with practice. Those who talk easily have simply had more practice. Group members will experience why interested listening and caring talk contribute to easy communication. Adolescents can learn to share these skills themselves as they enjoy receiving them from others.

Adolescents need give-and-take in their relationships. It does little good if one person does all the talking or all the listening in a relationship. This session encourages group members to select friends they can both talk to and listen to. Equip and pray with your students. Affirm the importance of sharing feelings and ideas, of understanding and being understood, of encouraging and receiving encouragement.

Goals:

The goals for the *leader* include
(1) guiding group members to express ideas about talking and listening;
(2) guiding them to model their talking and listening after Jesus' example;
(3) equipping group members to listen for, share, and respond to details.

The goals for the *group members* are that they will
(1) affirm the interdependence of listening and talking;
(2) tackle obstacles to communication;
(3) practice listening and talking skills.

Life Response:

Group members will use communication skills to more thoroughly and delightfully communicate with their friends.

Resource Materials:

___ Bibles
___ pens or pencils
___ one copy of *I Thought You Were My Friend!* for each member
___ posted signs that read: Agree, Disagree, Strongly Agree, Strongly Disagree.
___ building blocks, preferably with letters

 **HEARTBEAT**

As group members enter, point out the signs on the four walls: AGREE, DISAGREE, STRONGLY AGREE, STRONGLY DISAGREE and tell them to move to the sign that most closely matches how they feel about the statements you will read aloud. Read each of the following one at a time and wait until all have moved to a sign. (Call first on the smallest group to affirm their courage in choosing to stand alone or with the minority.) Invite one person from each group to tell why he or she chose that particular response. Read the next statement, have students move to their response, discuss the choices, and repeat the process until all the statements have been read. Allow each group member an equal amount of time to respond to questions. Afterward, point out that everyone's comments have shed light on the importance of talking and listening in friendships.

Say What You Believe

Do you strongly disagree (SD), disagree (D), agree (A), or strongly agree (SA) with each of these statements? Jot down a reason for your choice.

SD / D / A / SA 1. Listening is the most important factor in friendship.

☞ **[HELP: Listening is very important because true friends hear each other and value what the other says. But listening is only one of many other important qualities, such as showing interest and being kind. All of these qualities must be present in a strong friendship.]**

SD / D / A / SA 2. Each member of a friendship pair should speak about as much as they listen.

☞ [HELP: This is definitely true because give-and-take is vital to healthy friendships. However, some talk or listen more. Allow for differences. "About as much" is the key phrase.]

SD / D / A / SA 3. It is easier to listen than talk.

☞ [HELP: Listening can seem easier because you feel you're not "doing" anything. But good listening requires lots of doing: eye contact, nodding, saying "uh-huh," repeating what you hear. Good listening shows attention and care. Some find it easier to talk; others find it easier to listen.]

SD / D / A / SA 4. You tend to be either a good listener or a good talker.

☞ [HELP: Some people are naturally good at listening or talking. Both, however, are learned skills. Those who listen or talk well have likely had good models and lots of practice. Grow your listening and talking skills, and encourage your friends to do the same. You and your friends can learn to listen, learn to talk, and put them together to grow closeness.]

SD / D / A /SA 5. You must share feelings and ideas to be truly close.

☞ [HELP: Feelings and ideas do lead to deeper understanding and togetherness. But there are other important ways to grow close: working together on a project, sharing the same experiences at school or church, worshiping God together, going through a difficult experience together. Feelings and ideas show our hearts, but so do actions and attitudes.]

☞ [HINT: To continue the discussion, invite group members to suggest their own statements about talking and listening, statements that bring out many facets of the truths about listening and talking.]

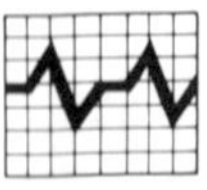 **LIFELINE**

Watch Good Listeners

Few skills are more important to the success of a friendship than mutual listening and talking. A friend who does all the talking keeps you from sharing your ideas, feelings, thoughts, worries, successes, pleasures, and pain. And a friend who does all the listening encourages you to stay centered on yourself and the things you're talking about.

So rather than grow a friendship that feeds your selfishness or squelches your need to share, find and grow close to friends who both listen and speak, and who give you the freedom to listen and speak. Let your friendships help each member feel confident about talking and committed to true listening.

How can you grow your talking and listening skills? Study Bible communication and watch good communicators. Write the name of someone who communicates well.

____

Then search Ephesians 4:25-32 for actions this good communicator does with his eyes, hands, head, heart, mouth, feet, knees, and more. Write these characteristics here:

____

☞ [HELP: Encourage group members to apply this passage to communication rather than simply write the actions. Examples: Instead of "true talk," write something like "This person *speaks truthfully* in kind, not cutting, ways"; Instead of "be nice," write, "This person is *kind and compassionate* because she stops what she's doing to look right at you when you talk."]

Tackle Talk Trouble

As you watch good communicators, tackle the obstacles that keep you from talking and listening well. Circle your greatest talk trouble.

Saying too much
    Saying too little
        Not speaking at the right times
            Putting people down
              Complaining
                Criticizing
                  Swearing
                  (other) _______________________

Decode below the following prescription for talk trouble and then tell how you'll apply it to solve any particular problem you have. To decode the prescription, place a vertical line at the end of each word. Then read it aloud and find the passage in your Bible:

BEIMITATORSOFGODTHEREFOREASDEARLYLOVEDCHIL-
DRENANDLIVEALIFEOFLOVEJUSTASCHRISTLOVEDUS
ANDGAVEHIMSELFUPFORUSASAFRAGRANTOFFERING
ANDSACRIFICETOGODEPHESIANS5:1-2.

Very simply, the prescription is to imitate Jesus. How will you apply this prescription to the talk trouble you circled above?

Imitating Jesus brings a life of love. How did Jesus talk to others?

How did Jesus listen?

IMPORTANT: Solving talk trouble is seldom accomplished in a single try. Keep working as you consciously let God transform your talk.

☞ **[HELP: The prescription is Ephesians 5:1-2. Encourage group members to keep their Bibles open to it as they answer questions. Have them give more than one example for each question. Remember, Jesus didn't talk or listen in only one way: Jesus *spoke* soothingly to the children who came to Him (Matt. 18:1-6); He spoke appreciatively to the woman who washed His feet (Luke 7:44-48); He spoke to forgive the same woman (v. 48); Jesus spoke sternly to the Pharisees when they acted hypocritically and taught false things about God (Matt. 23:23-33). He spoke in many other ways.**

Jesus *listened* by asking questions that led the person to seek and find the truth (Matt. 16:13-16); He affirmed wise answers and insights that He heard (Matt. 16:17-20); Jesus listened for single voices and needs within a crowd (Mark 5:24-34); Jesus listened by getting quiet when speaking would only stir up the situation—He used quiet to calm things down (John 8:2-11); Jesus listened to both what people said and what they meant (8:3-6; Mark 10:26-31); Jesus listened to answer people's deeper questions (10:17-21; 41-45); He listened in more ways.

Jesus' talking and listening were good models of love because He matched what He said and acted according to the need at hand. He also showed loyalty to God in the way He spoke and in choosing the words He spoke. Guide group members to notice examples of this and to name ways they could imitate Him. For example, they might not call friends "whitewashed tombs" (Matt. 22:27), but they could firmly but respectfully communicate that wrong behavior is wrong. They would not heal a friend in a crowd, but they could keep "looking around" for pain and respond to it (Mark 5:30-32).]

Avoid the Traps

Imitating Jesus is the key to good talking and listening in friendships. But the devil sets many traps to keep you from it. Read 1 Timothy 6:4-5 to underline the talk traps in your Bible. Then complete this chart:

The Trap	**When I Have Been or Am Likely to Get Caught in This Trap**
1. Conceit	
2. Not understanding what really matters	
3. Unhealthy interest in controversies	
4. Quarrels	
5. Envy (jealousy)	
6. Strife (bitter conflict)	
7. Malicious talk (gossip; spreading dirt)	
8. Evil suspicions (looking for the worst)	
9. Constant friction between people	
10. Corrupt mind (believing and living by lies)	
11. Wrong view of godliness	

What instruction in Ephesians 4:25–5:2 could you to avoid or crawl out of a trap that entangles your commu-nication?

☞ **[HELP: Invite each group member to comment on a different trap. Direct them to quote a phrase from Ephesians 4:25 — 5:2 and to be specific in their examples. For example: "I'll respond to gossip by *compassionately* saying something good about the person. I'll refuse to spread gossip, even if true, because it would *grieve the Holy Spirit.*"]**

 **BODYLIFE**

Bring Care to Your Listening

Because listening and speaking are skills, you can become a better communicator with each conversation. Understand both feelings and ideas as you listen. Respond in ways that help. To practice understanding feelings and ideas, ask:

1. What feelings does your friend have if she says . . .
"I failed the test. It wouldn't be so bad if I hadn't studied for three hours. And the people who didn't study at all made higher grades than me. I don't see why I try at all. It was a stupid test."

What response does your friend want and need from you?
☐ Just to understand.
☐ To feel the feelings she feels.
☐ To tell about a time when you felt similarly.
☐ To listen more while she figures out what to do next.
☐ To give advice that encourages her to discover and think through her options.
☐ To take a turn talking while she listens.
☐ To share biblical principles or Bible passages.
☐ ____

Why did you choose the answer you did? _______________

____

☞ **[HELP: This friend feels sad, discouraged, and stupid. She wishes her hard work had paid off. She wonders if** she's just dumb—why else would she have failed the test? If she isn't stupid, why did she do so poorly on the test? She feels like it's just not worth trying.

This friend first needs understanding and empathy. She needs to know that her feelings make sense, that somebody knows how she feels. She also needs to know that she is an intelligent, valuable person. You might communicate this with "That has happened to me before. It feels rotten doesn't it?" OR "It happens to even the smartest people." Statements like these will likely encourage your friend to talk some more.

You might want to further affirm her intelligence with words like, "Some tests are different than you expect or are poorly worded. No matter how much you study, it's hard to do well. Maybe this test can show you the kind of questions your teacher asks so you can do better next time."

After listening some more, you can offer ideas for what to do now and next time. You could encourage her to find God's solution with a question or two: "Will there be another test you can use to pull up your grade?" "Is there a way to retake it?" "Can you do extra credit?" "What do you think you should do next time?" Bible insights to share include: the Lord is near to and can heal the brokenhearted (Pss. 34:18; 147:3).

Listen before you suggest. It's better to say too little than appear to give overly simple answers to a situation that matters a lot to your friend. Sometimes what your friend wants is not what she needs (she might want you to feel sorry for her rather than find a solution). But if you know both what she wants and needs, you can better meet the needs.]

2. What ideas does your friend have if he says *"I'd like to enter the art contest but I'm afraid I won't win. I'd really like to submit one of those horse paintings I've been working on. What do you think I should do?"*

What response does your friend want and need from you?

☐ To encourage him to talk more about why he wants to enter.

☐ To tell him reasons he could win.

☐ To help him see the benefits of entering the contest, even if he doesn't win.

☐ To listen more while he figures out what to do next.

☐ To ask him to show you the horse paintings.

☐ To attend the contest to support and cheer him on.

☐ To share biblical principles or Bible passages.

☐ ______________________________________

Why? ______________________________________

☞ **[HELP: This friend wants to enter a contest he's never tried before. He likely has other ideas he has not yet expressed. He may be testing the waters to see if you really want to hear his idea. If so, he'll definitely want you to ask more about why he wants to enter. Asking to see the horse paintings would also show you are very interested in hearing more about his idea. Avoid promising him a win. You don't know what will happen, and it's best to focus on what a good experience it would be for him to enter. Possible Bible insights to share include doing your best for God (Col. 3:23).**

Rather than assume you know your friend's ideas, ask questions and then listen with interest. Examples include: "What else have you thought about it?" "What excites you most about the possibilities?" "What first got you thinking about this?"]

Now choose a partner in the group and share both ideas and feelings with each other. Choose something you've been thinking about recently. After both of you share, tell your partner the ideas and feelings you heard.

1. What made you a good listener according to your partner?

2. What made it easy to listen to your partner?

3. How could you have listened better?

Bring Care to Your Speech

Just as you want to know and understand your friend's feelings and ideas, good friends want to know and understand your feelings and ideas. Ponder the last time you went through a happy, sad, victorious, or discouraging time. Draw or describe the feelings you had about your experience. Write every feeling you can remember without stopping to analyze them:

What ideas, hopes, dreams, and facts did and do you have about that experience? Let your ideas, hopes, dreams, and facts flow, but don't take the time to evaluate each one.

☞ **[HELP: One value of writing without stopping to evaluate is that more feelings, ideas, hopes, dreams, and facts have time to come. If we stop to evaluate, we may forget the other ideas we wanted to put down. Yet if we speak without thinking, we may hurt ourselves or someone else. So a balance is needed. This exercise helps group members practice that balance.]**

Now write what you'll say to your friend about your feelings, ideas, dreams, and facts. Use wholesome, rather than unwholesome talk, honest rather than what-you-think-your-friend-wants-you-to-say talk (Eph. 4:25, 29). Now is the time to think through and evaluate:

How does it help to think through what to say before you say it?

What do you want your friend to do as a result of what you've shared?

- ☐ Just to understand
- ☐ To feel the feelings I feel
- ☐ To tell me a time he or she felt similarly
- ☐ To listen more while I figure out what to do next
- ☐ To share advice that encourages me to discover and think through my options
- ☐ To take a turn talking while I listen
- ☐ To share biblical principles or Bible passages
- ☐ ____

Why? ____

Life Response

☞ **[HINT: Display a set of building blocks. Ask: Why are interested listening and caring talk building blocks to close friendships? Tell group members to imagine that some of the blocks represent listening skills and other blocks talking skills. For each block present, have a group member name a listening or talking skill that builds friendship. If you have blocks with letters on the side, suggest they start their reason with a letter on the block. Direct group members to build a building as they name reasons.]**

Friendships are built a block at a time. Imagine your favorite friendship as a building built with listening and talking blocks.

1. How do interested listening and caring talk build your friendship?

2. What will make the building blocks of your friendship stable?

3. What forces will threaten to knock it down?

4. How will you listen and talk to keep it steady during winds of trouble?

☞ [HELP: Additional Life Responses to include if time allows or to suggest for home follow-through:
1. As you read Scripture this week, notice ways God, or God in Jesus Christ, both listens and speaks. Imitate Him in your friendships.
2. Speak to someone you have never spoken to before. Let your words communicate care or give confidence in a new way.
3. Listen to someone you have never listened to before. Find the wisdom in the words and ideas they share. Tell him or her what you hear.
4. Make sure everyone in your age group receives a warm welcome as they come to Sunday School, small group, or another meeting at church. Notice the loving power of simple, caring words.]

What's Next?

When might you be a fair-weather friend? How do you stick around and care for your friend, even when it's painful?

FOUR

Be There for Your Friends

SESSION OVERVIEW

Purpose:

This session challenges group members to go through sad times with their friends, even when it's difficult for them. Such times include grief, serious or life-threatening illnesses, temporary or long-lasting disabilities, accidents, and hospitalization.

Needs:

Even the most caring people tend to pull back when their friends hit a crisis. They don't know what to do or say, so they do nothing. This session attempts to prevent this compound tragedy by equipping group members to care, even when care doesn't come naturally. Group members can discover that care during crisis is not all that different than care during any life experience. It's just harder because they hurt for their friends.

Many friends try to avoid this pain by staying away and claiming that they *can't* handle it. But the problem is not that they *can't* handle it; it's that they *won't* handle it. Besides, the pain won't go away by itself. People still hurt. So friends might as well share the pain together. Encourage group members to choose to go through pain with friends because they love them, not because it's easy. Staying close enables friends to handle their crises.

Good friends have fun, study, talk about things that matter, solve problems, do chores, grow in Christ, and are there for each other. These shared experiences form the foundation for being helpful when the hard times come. The most helpful friends are those who were already close before the crisis. But there are definite exceptions to this rule. A friend you barely know can become precious simply because he or she goes out of the way to care. So group members need not hesitate to show care if they have met someone only recently.

Goals:

The goals for the *leader* include
(1) guiding group members to recognize that caring during crisis is motivated by choice and by love, not feeling;
(2) citing specific ways group members can stay close to their friends;
(3) equipping group members to commit to specific caring actions.

The goals for the *group members* are that they will
(1) pinpoint a way they currently back away from friends;
(2) affirm sad times as a part of life that are easier when faced together;
(3) prepare a specific way they will care for others both now and in the future.

Life Response:

Group members will choose to walk with friends through pain because they care about the friend, not because it's easy.

Resource Materials:

___ Bibles

___ **pens or pencils**
___ **one copy of *I Thought You Were My Friend!* for each member**

 **HEARTBEAT**

As group members enter, invite each to give you a one-word description of crisis ("sad," "painful," "life-threatening," etc.). Then pair members and challenge them to create the longest list of crises. To capture interest, explain that each *crisis listed* must start with the letter the previous ended with. Samples: *Car acciden*T . . . *Test I faile*D . . . *Dumped by stead*Y . . . *Yelled at by abusive parent*S . . . *Shot at schoo*L . . . *Learned friend has cance*R . . . *Really close person die*D . . . *Dying mysel*F . . . *Flood destroyed hom*E . . . *Ever-worsening disabilit*Y . . . *Your family is against Christianity* . . .

Notice the Crises

Choose or write your favorite definition for CRISIS:

- [ ] deeply sad event
- [ ] something bad that happens
- [ ] an intensely painful time
- [ ] attack on God's goodness

- [ ] disturbance to life
- [ ] death or life-threatening event
- [ ] something requiring hospitalization
- [ ] __________

We all wish we could make crises go away. But sad times are a part of life. Our friends will face injuries, death, disabilities, illnesses, consequences of poor choices, and other tragedies. And they need our help. These problems matter because they matter to our friends. Name three crises your friends have experienced or could experience:

1.
2.
3.

Hold the Umbrella during Foul Weather

Some friends, even sincere ones, run and hide when problems come. They claim they "can't handle it." We call these fair-weather friends. But to show true love, a friend will put up his umbrella and face the storm with his hurting friend. It's not easy, but it's right. Nobody wants to go through rough times, but loving friends do it for the sake of the one who hurts. Notice where it's hard for you, and then move past that difficulty to care anyway. During what bad time would you tend to flee from your friend?

☐ when friend is diagnosed with a serious disease
☐ when he or she has an accident that results in disability
☐ serious illness in the friend's family
☐ when friend has been hospitalized
☐ my friend's loved one has died
☐ my friend may die soon
☐ when my friend cries
☐ when I feel like crying
☐ ______________________________

Read Proverbs 17:17. What might persuade you to put up your umbrella and care?
☐ I'd think about how I'd want to be treated.
☐ I'd remember that my friend has no choice about going through the bad time.
☐ I'd remember that my friend needs me.
☐ I'd focus on my friend's feelings, not my feelings.
☐ I'd know that God will empower me.
☐ I'd recall that it's easier to go through hard times together than alone.
☐ ______________________________

 **LIFELINE**

Don't Miss the Times of Your Life

Good friends work, study, talk, listen, comfort, and support each other. All these contribute to mutual growth in

Christ. Search Ecclesiastes 3:1-8 for three times you share well with your friends:

1.

2.

3.

Now using the same passage, search for three life experiences you avoid sharing with your friends:

1.

2.

3.

We often find it easier to share the joys than the sorrows. But sorrows are as much a part of life as the joys. And caring during those times may be more important because few are willing to do so.

Caring for a friend during hard times doesn't mean you have to do the impossible. You don't have to look at the needle, but you can go along to the doctor's office. You don't have to hold back tears because your friend will be glad you care enough to cry. You don't have to figure out just what to do, you simply have to go. You can do it because God will give you three things. Find these in your Bible.

God will give me _____________ (Philippians 4:13).

God will give me _____________ (Matthew 10:20).

God will give me _____________ (Psalm 32:8).

☞ **[HELP: Some answers might include STRENGTH or POWER (Phil. 4:13); WORDS or HIS SPIRIT (Matt. 10:20); INSTRUCTION or RIGHT ACTIONS (Ps. 32:8). Welcome other wise answers.]**

Caring for a friend during crisis boils down to taking action. Fill in the verbs in Hebrews 10:24-25 to discover four key actions to being a friend who stays with friends through easy and hard times:

"And let us __________ how we may __________ one another on toward love and good deeds. Let us __________ __________ __________ together as some are in the habit of doing; but let us __________ one another — and all the more as you see the Day approaching" (Hebrews 10:24-25).

☞ [HELP: Answers from the NIV are: consider, spur, not give up meeting, encourage. Assign each group member one action and direct them to speak for 30 seconds on how it would help a friend during a crisis. For example, a friend could spur on a friend to tone up muscles after surgery. Ask: Why would you want a friend to do this for you? Why do you want to do it for a friend?]

Bring up Your Grades

Now return to Ecclesiastes 3:1-8 for specific ways you can consider, spur on, not give up meeting together, and encourage your friends during crises. Give yourself a letter grade from A to F on how well you have shared these life experiences with your friends.

Let God be your teacher and invite Him to give you His power, words, and actions for the present and future. Write God's advice in the teacher's comment space that follows this list.

Grade   *Subject (from Ecclesiastes 3:1-8)*

________   Celebrating birthdays
________   Supporting a friend who has lost someone close
________   Planting (growing something good in your friend's life)

________ Uprooting and tearing down (changing something bad in your friend)

________ Healing (spiritual, emotional, physical, relational) a friend's problems

________ Building (relationships, Christian growth) with a friend

________ Weeping with my friend

________ Laughing with my friend (not at my friend)

________ Mourning along with my friend

________ Dancing and otherwise rejoicing with my friend

________ Embracing at the right time

________ Searching for what my friend needs

________ Giving up those things that do our friendship no good

________ Keeping up with each other's needs

________ Throwing away my desires or comforts to help my friend

________ Tearing (confronting a friend who is acting selfishly)

________ Mending (healing a broken or wounded relationship with a friend)

________ Being silent when silence is needed

________ Speaking when words will help my friend

________ Loving what needs loving

________ Hating those actions that should be hated (acts of Satan)

________ Working toward peace

TEACHER'S COMMENTS:

This student does especially well at ______ by ________

    and especially well at ______ by __________

    and especially well at ______ by __________

This student could bring up his/her grade

    for ______ by ____________________

    for ______ by ____________________

    for ______ by ____________________

☞ [HINT: Invite group members to fill out their report cards privately and then talk to each other about the grades they gave themselves. They may want to reveal some information and keep some private; give and receive advice; offer ideas for doing better the next grading period. Do this sharing in pairs or trios. Then mix up the groups and repeat. Notice the support that develops. Point out that when they share this way, they are following Hebrews 10:24–25.]

BODYLIFE

Do More than the Send-a-Card-and-Visit Standard

What two things do you first think of doing when a friend is sick or injured?

1. _________________________   2. _________________________

You likely think about sending a card or visiting. Both of these matter greatly, but there is much more friends can do for each other. Think of make-it-through-the-pain actions you can take while you're with a friend. After reading the samples, come up with your own ideas:

- Run interference for a friend who's been out of school by letting everybody know where she's been and what she needs now. By answering questions now, you'll make it easier for your friend to return.
- Have wheelchair races with your friend who's adapting to a wheelchair.
- Help your recovering friend with his therapy by doing exercises with him, by counting, or by doing whatever he asks you to do.
- Shop for cute hats for your soon-to-be-bald-from-chemo friend.
- Complement an aspect of your burned friend's appearance.
- When your friend's swimsuit strap breaks and she has to wear a T-shirt, wear a T-shirt over your suit too.

- ____
- ____

And during the times your physical presence isn't possible or helpful, you can still care. Find another way:

- When your friend is in intensive care, only family members are admitted. Ask about sending a taped message or a teddy bear instead.
- When your friend has had a painful surgery and is sleepy or hurting, send balloons or a special video she can watch when awake.
- When your friend has had a bone marrow transplant and cannot have visitors, gather 10 to 20 friends to each write a "What-I-appreciate-about-you" letter. Give them to nurses who can deliver one a day.
- When your friend lives in a different city, send photographs of fun times you've had together to cover her wall at home or in the hospital. Or send a big box with a present for every day of the recovery time.
- When _______________________________; I can _______________________________ instead.
- When _______________________________; I can _______________________________ instead.

Let Each Other Know What You Need
One reason friends don't help each other during hard times is they don't know what to do. Prevent this problem by using your listening and talking skills to find out what your friend wants and needs (recall session 3).

Sometimes we think a friend should just know how another friend feels and what the other needs. But no one can read minds. Instead we've got to ask questions, listen, and love. Invite your friend to tell you the details about the surgery or procedure. Ask your friend or your friend's family to name specific things you can do. Offer to do your friend's chores and other practical things, as well as to give care directly to your friend. The following is a list of questions you might ask a hurting friend:

"How are you feeling about all this?"

"What can I do to help?"

"Can I shop for something specific?"

"Can I fill in for you at church or work? What home chores I can do?"

"What homework assignments or daily notes can I get for you?"

"What do you want to know about what's happening at school?"

"Would you like to hear about what we've been doing at church?"

"Let me know when you want me to go; or if you need me to stay longer."

"____"

"____"

In the same way, when you're the hurting one, say what you need:

"Would you answer the phone while you're here?"

"Will you let people know _______?"

"Would you mind checking with my teachers daily for assignments?"

"Can you put a carbon under your notes so I'll have a copy?"

"I know this sounds strange, but could you scratch my back right there?"

"Can I tell you the details of the surgery? I've got to tell somebody."

"____"

"____"

LISTENING not only helps you find out what your friend needs. It also meets a need itself. Few people are willing to hear sad experiences. Be the friend who listens no matter how painful the situation being described. Remember to let your friend tell you how he feels. Don't assume you know how your friend feels or why. Your friend's quietness in the hospital may not mean anger or depression. Quietness can mean calmness or simple sleepiness. Ask so you'll know.

TALKING shows your friend she still matters to you. Talking about the crisis shows you care about the details. Talking about things besides the crisis shows you still value your friendship, that you believe your friend has a life beyond the crisis, and that she can still participate in that life. Don't overwhelm your friend with chatter. Let talking and listening be mutual.

How else might LISTENING and TALKING help during crises?

When is it best to talk about the crisis? To forget the crisis for a time to focus on something else?

Spell What You'll Do

Another way to prevent the I-don't-know-how-to-help problem is to list in advance some things you could do. Together with the group, complete this alphabet with actions you'll do the next time your friend encounters a crisis such as grief, serious illness, accident, surgery, a sudden or suddenly worsened disability, or a life-threatening disease.

A

B

C

*D*eliver a thoughtful present to the friend in the hospital

E

F

G

H

I

J

*K*eep on being interested even if the crisis has gone on a long time.

L

*M*oney used to buy fun gifts or an item my friend needs

N

O

P

Q

R

S

T

U

V

*W*ant to hear the details

X

Y

Z

☞　[HINT: Divide into teams of two and challenge each team to address a different kind of crisis. Then combine ideas so each letter has multiple ideas. Samples: *A*sk how it's going and listen; *B*ible verse a day (choose a verse for every day in the hospital so that he or she can open one each morning); *C*ards signed by friends or gather a card from each friend; *D*iary given so friend can write or draw feelings and ideas; *E*xtra special bubble baths or soaps; *F*ilms of friends saying get-well or we-care messages (can be photographs, videos, or poster-sized enlarged photos; *G*et homework daily at school and take it to hospital, help teach it if needed; *H*elium balloons, perhaps signed on the back by friends; *I*nterested in the details, not grossed out; *J*ust as willing to let friend cry as laugh; *K*eep asking about long-term challenges as well as everyday stuff like homework and crushes; *L*eave stuff in front or back door so he or she will get it after coming home from a day at hospital or school; *M*essages on answering machine; *N*otes taken in class while friend is away; *O*ther people informed with prayer requests and needs (then coordinate getting those needs met); *P*resent with friend when has to go through rough procedure; *Q*uestions about what's next; *R*ead to and with; *S*ay why you like the friend; *T*ake his favorite foods (or freeze if he can't eat them now); *U*nderstand what details mean and ask him or her if I don't understand; *V*isit in the hospital or home; *W*eekly contact in some way; *X*cited when good happens like an illness going into remission; *Y*ou tell me and I'll remember; *Z*any presents—a squirt gun and crazy glasses make hospital stay more entertaining.]

Life Response

You have many resources with which to help your friends in crisis. Name a way you could use each of these to show care for your friend:

telephone:
car:
pencil or pen:
conversation:
money:

other friends:
camera:
cassette recorder:

REMEMBER: You can never say "I can't handle it" because God will give you the power (Phil. 4:13), words (Matt. 10:20), and actions (Ps. 32:8). You can say "I refuse to handle it," but it's always better to say, "I will handle it, no matter how hard, for the sake of my friend."

☞ **[HELP: Additional Life Responses to include if time allows or to suggest for home follow-through:**

1. Name a friend (or acquaintance) who is going through a crisis right now. Talk with God about the specific action He wants you to take. Complete that friendship action within the next three days.

2. Shop for some gifts you could give to friends in the hospital—good possibilities include cuddly teddy bears, undated diaries/journals, funny slippers, over-size cards, fun-to-do-in-a-hospital-bed projects. Keep these, with wrapping paper, in a special place in your closet so you can take them to the hospital without spending precious time at the store that could be spent caring for that person.

3. Invite a friend who has been through a past crisis to tell what really helped her. Ask also what didn't help her. Ask what no one did that she wishes a person had done. Be the one to do the helpful things next time.]

What's Next?
What is integrity and what difference does it make in friendship?

FIVE

Buy More than a Designer Label

SESSION OVERVIEW

Purpose:

True quality comes from the workmanship, not the label. This session encourages group members to let God design them and to grow close to friends who live this same commitment.

Needs:

Adolescents know what makes a good friend. They want real people who are interesting and loving. They want to wrestle the questions of life and faith with people they can trust. Then they want to live the truth with people they genuinely enjoy.

Group members know that friendships like these go far beyond the surface. The more you get to know someone with the characteristics of a good friend, the more of these good qualities you can see. But surface labels can have power even over those who recognize the value of in-depth friendships. Their minds tell them that labels such as looks, status, and popularity are just labels, but their hearts tell them these people must be somehow better. Too often they seek the company of "label people" and reject the more caring friends. Interestingly, even the label "Christian" is not always reliable. Just because someone wears the label, attends church, and talks the talk doesn't mean that person obeys God in daily life. We've got to see the Designer's work in actions and attitudes.

This session focuses on integrity—a consistent and demonstrated loyalty to God and people. It stresses the importance of friends who not only wear the label "Christian," but who let God design their actions, attitudes, and words. He is the true Designer, the Provider of the quality we want in friendships. His is the design label we want on our friendships. Group members will commit to be people of integrity themselves, as well as to notice and grow close to other people of integrity. They will notice when they seek out labels rather than quality, so they can deliberately choose quality. They will then wrestle with ways they can give this kind of quality to their friends now and in the future.

Goals:

The goals for the *leader* include

(1) guiding group members to recognize that they value faith in friendship;

(2) guiding group members to embrace God as their friendship designer;

(3) equipping group members to apply God's truth to tough situations.

The goals for the *group members* are that they will

(1) notice that faith really does impact friendship;

(2) commit to do faith-based friendship actions as guided by the Designer;

(3) name ways to show a consistent and demonstrated loyalty to God and people in their friendships.

Life Response:

Group members will invite God to design their actions, attitudes, and words so they and their friends can grow strong.

Resource Materials:
____ Bibles
____ pens or pencils
____ one copy of *I Thought You Were My Friend!* for each member
____ masking tape and paper cut into the shape of labels

HEARTBEAT

As group members enter, direct them to complete and discuss the first two questions. Then explain what integrity is before doing the rest of the section.

Notice Why It Matters

What matters most in your friendships? As a Christian, your first response should be the faith you share in common. But as you know, shared faith doesn't always make a friendship. Some wear the label "Christian" without letting God design their actions, attitudes, and words. Describe a time a Christian friend didn't act like a Christian (no names or identifying details please):

What bugged you about this? Why does it matter when Christians say one thing and do another? Or act one way at church and another at school?

Getting frustrated and angry about these actions helps us realize the truth: Faith is not just something we talk about and believe, it's something we must show in life. It really does matter how we treat people. Being who God wants you to be makes a real difference in friendship. We call this integrity—living our faith. Choose your favorite synonyms for integrity:

completeness　　　　　　*undivided loyalty*
character　　　　　　　　*blamelessness*

honesty　　　　　　　*honor*
principle　　　　　　*decency*
genuineness　　　　*commitment*

A Christian with integrity displays undivided loyalty to God. As a consequence, this friend treats people as God would. We can summarize these two actions by saying a person of integrity shows consistent and demonstrated loyalty to God and people. Complete these sentences to explain why integrity is important to your friendships:

A friend with integrity—a consistent and demonstrated loyalty to God and people—makes me feel . . .

A friend with integrity frees me to be my best self by . . .

A friend with integrity helps me live my faith by . . .

A friend with integrity is also important because . . .

LIFELINE
Buy Designer Actions

Friends with integrity stay with us through thick and thin, care for us as God would, and free us to be all God calls us to be. But most of what we see contradicts this. Our society laughs at sarcasm, wrongdoing, and self-centeredness. Movies that portray betrayal, abandonment, and controlling others do better at the box office than those that show loyalty, genuineness, and freeing each other to grow. Many of us feel like we've got to swim upstream to build a solid and caring friendship. Go ahead and swim—if salmon can succeed, so can we!

Deliberately choose actions that match God, your Designer. Choose to treat your friends like He would. Show interest, spend time together, enjoy and love each other, honor God in all this. Let God teach you how.

Start by locating the following friendship actions in Galatians 6:1-10. Write the verse where each action is found. Then write its opposite to help you understand how to do and not do it.

Designer Friendship Actions   ***Opposite Action***

v.____: If someone is caught
in a sin, restore him gently.

v.____: Carry each other's burdens.

v.____: Test your own actions
without . . . comparing
to somebody else.

v.____: Carry your own load.

v.____: Share all good things
with teachers.

v.____: See reality rather than
try to mock God.

v.____: Refuse to sow to please
your sinful nature.

v.____: Act and speak to
please the Spirit.

v.____: Do not grow weary
in doing good.

v.____: Do good to all people.

☞   **[HELP: Stress that writing opposites is a Bible study
method that helps us know how to obey the verse be-**

cause it shows what *not* to do. Sample opposites: v. 1—gossip about the one who sins, get back at him, restore him with shame; v. 2—assume it's your friend's problem, say you can't handle it; v. 4—compete, compare self to others, assume superior to some, assume inferior to others; v. 5—dump on others, be lazy, not do your part, refuse to do the hard stuff; v. 6—(explain that Christians were responsible for the monetary support of their teachers) fail to appreciate a friend who taught you about God, give teachers a hard time during class, vote for no or low raises for paid staff; v. 7—mock God through ridiculing people; pretend God doesn't exist; pretend "It's OK to do wrong because God will understand and forgive me"; v. 8—pretend you can do what you want without hurting anyone; assume you can get away with wrong; v. 8—ignore the Spirit; pretend God doesn't care what you do as long as you go to church; v. 9—assume it's someone else's turn to help; assume you've done your part; v. 10—talk only to certain people; assume only some deserve your time and attention.]

1. God is our Designer and knows best how to grow our friendships. Choose a friendship action from the chart and tell how it grows friendship:

2. How does friendship suffer when you fail to do that friendship action? (Use the opposite action you wrote.)

3. Each person must decide for himself or herself to follow the Designer. As we encourage wrongdoing friends to follow the Designer, what danger do we face, according to verse 1?

4. Why do friendships need both verse 2 and verse 5?

5. Who can never be fooled according to verse 7? When have you tried?

☞ **[HELP: Answers for last three: Verse 1 warns we may do wrong. Ask: How do you help a struggling friend without being drawn into wrong? When have you or someone you know been drawn into wrong? What advice do you have for avoiding this? (Suggest that you may want to spend less time — or no time alone — with that friend.) Verses 2 and 5 encourage mutual care and interdependence. This keeps a person from taking advantage of a friendship and gives balance between giving and receiving. Verse 7 explains that God cannot be mocked. Ask: Why do we try to mock God? What makes us feel like we're getting away with this kind of behavior?]**

Let God Design Your Words

We've studied how to act. How you talk also matters. God, our Designer, cares about what we say to and about people. Proverbs 12:18 says: "__________ words pierce like a __________, but the tongue of the __________ brings __________."

Proverbs 16:24 calls designer words honey words. These words are "__________ to the soul and __________ to the bones."

What words do this for you? Write at least five sweet and healing words/phrases you can use to care about your friends like God does:

1.
2.
3.
4.
5.

☞ **[HELP: 12:18 — Reckless, sword, wise, healing. 16:24 — sweet, healing. (Some group members may think of overly syrupy words when they hear *honey* and *sweet*. Invite them to name other adjectives for godly words, perhaps those in Eph. 4:29.) Sample phrases: "It's good to see you"; "You understand"; "Thanks for listening"; "Tell me how it went"; "I like the way you treat people"; "Your smile makes me happy"; "I'm glad I know you."]**

Using designer words when talking directly to people can be hard. But using designer words when talking about them can be even harder. Because we enjoy telling stories with friends, gossip and slander are tempting sins. Bad situations appear to make good stories. Why do stories of good and right make the best tales according to Proverbs 26:18-28, especially verses 27-28?

Practice telling interesting and fun stories by noticing how people live according to God, the Designer. Write a story of someone you know who does neat things in friendship:

☞ **[HINT: Invite each member to take turns telling about a real person in the community who lives with integrity. Avoid superstars, athletes, TV personalities, and famous pastors. Encourage everyday people they know.]**

Now get even more specific by telling a story about a person in this small group. How have you seen the person on your left show integrity, a consistent and demonstrated loyalty to God and people, in this group during the past five sessions?

How is talking about the good people do more interesting than gossip?

When is it bragging? When does it encourage both you and your friend to live faith in friendship?

 **BODYLIFE**

Shop for Quality

Friendship with integrity is not a second-rate substitute for looks, status, and popularity. Instead, it's the first-class way of replacing shallowness and surface appearances with enjoyable and lasting relationships. But even though we know this in our minds, our feelings can convince us that people labeled "good-looking" and "popular" are really better. We find ourselves seeking these people and rejecting the more genuine friends. When are you drawn to each of these labels and why?

Good looks:

Popularity/Status:

Brains:

Athletic ability:

Fame or fortune:

Political power:

A person with the above label(s) is not automatically a quality person. Equally important, a person with this label(s) is not automatically shallow. What actions or attitudes might show true quality under each label?

Name at least two ways you seek friends who are Designer-made, who not only wear the label "Christian," but who let God design their actions, attitudes, and words:

1.

2.

Work out the Hard Parts

Living as a designer Christian includes not only how you choose to live, but how you respond to others' choices. This can be really tough, but God will guide you as He guided people in the Bible. He has also given us Himself as a model of how to live on earth. Talk with others in the group about how God would guide you to respond with integrity, a consistent and demonstrated loyalty to God and people, in situations like:

A. Katrina recently realized that her friend has been smoking and selling marijuana. Katrina feels that the problem is not the drug but her friend's loneliness and discouragement. Because marijuana is illegal and dangerous, Katrina wonders if she should go to the law or a counselor. But an arrest could make her friend feel even more lonely and discouraged. Katrina wants to do what would help her friend stop for good, to help her friend turn to God, rather than drugs, for power.

Katrina can respond with integrity (demonstrated loyalty to God and people) by . . .

This will be difficult for Katrina because . . .

But it will be possible because . . .

B. Jerome's coach wants him to use steroids to build mass and muscle strength. Jerome knows the dangers but also hopes to get a sports scholarship to pay for college. He struggles not only with the physical dangers the drug can produce but with the moral implications of using it— how strong an athlete will he really be if he depends on a drug? Can he take pride in his accomplishments if they are not really his? He asked the coach if he could work out extra rather than use the steroids, a way that Daniel might have responded (see Daniel 1:11-16). The coach, however, didn't seem receptive.

Jerome can respond with integrity (demonstrated loyalty to God and people) by . . .

This will be difficult for Jerome because . . .

But it will be possible because . . .

C. Lakisha is involved with many clubs and sports at school. She believes each gives her an opportunity to demonstrate Christlikeness to a different group. Lakisha attends Sunday morning Bible study and worship every week. In fact, if her team plays on a Sunday, Lakisha chooses to attend church. Lakisha misses most Wednesday night and Sunday night youth meetings. Lakisha's minister has come to her about her "lack of church involvement." When Lakisha tried to explain that she attends every Sunday and can't come more because of sports and school, her minister said, "If you're too busy for God, you're too busy." Lakisha believes God is not limited to the four walls of a church building. She sees every day as His.

Lakisha can respond with integrity (demonstrated loyalty to God and people) by . . .

This will be difficult for Lakisha because . . .

But it will be possible because . . .

D. Nicholas has one teacher who challenges his faith continually. He especially provokes Nicholas when he answers a question using Bible words or Bible truth. Lately the teacher has been countering almost everything Nicholas says. Nicholas can't tell if the teacher really wants to know more about Christianity or wants to prove that Christianity is wrong. And if the teacher thinks Christianity is wrong, why is he so threatened by it? Nicholas is working on his own attitude and words in case they come across as confrontational. And Nicholas works extra hard to be certain what he says is true. He wonders if he should be more quiet or more vocal in class.

Nicholas can respond with integrity (demonstrated loyalty to God and people) by . . .

This will be difficult for Nicholas because . . .

But it will be possible because . . .

☞ **[HELP: Encourage group members to model their actions after Jesus and others in the Bible who obeyed God. Direct them to seek God's answer rather than what looks like the answer. Following are two sample responses for each of the situations described above: For Katrina—Jesus' forgiveness of Mary, who later became a devout follower (see Luke 7:36-50 and John 11:1-3). Note that she stopped her sinful behavior; Jesus' encouragement to follow laws of God and government in Mark 12:14-17 (notice the word *integrity* in verse 14); for Jerome: Daniel in 1:3-20; Shadrach, Meshach, and Abednego in Daniel 3:1-30; for Lakisha— Jesus and the Pharisees in Matthew 12:1-13, and the command in Hebrews 10:24-25; for Nicholas—Jesus' response to the people who were open to him in such passages as John 3:1-21 and 19:39 and closed to His message in such passages as John 8:3-11 and Mark 14:61-63; Jesus' silence when people challenged him in passages like Mark 14:53-61. Encourage members to do their own Bible searching.]**

Life Response

As you live as a designer Christian, be sure you treat yourself with integrity. This includes valuing yourself and being honest enough to notice your weak points. When you notice an area of hypocrisy, correct it. When you discover that your talk doesn't match your walk, bring both in line with God's standards. God will give you the power and the strategies to do this. Write an improvement God wants you to make in your friendship actions:

Return to Galatians 6:1-10 and make a label for yourself that names the action you most want people to notice about the way you treat them. Maybe you want to treat everyone as a person of value. Verse 10 would be your label. Put the Bible phrase into your own words:

☞ **[HINT: Give group members tape and paper and direct them to tape the labels to a label on their clothes (inside collar, on back of a shoe, on pocket, etc.) Examples: Steadily Do Good (Gal. 6:9); Burden Bearer (Gal. 6:2).]**

☞ **[HELP: Additional Life Responses to include if time allows or to suggest for home follow-through:**
1. With what words, besides *designer Christian* and *integrity*, would you stress the need for faith in friendship? Use these words to write an article or story about how to live faith in friendship.
2. Consider a person you have ignored in the past who may be a solid and interesting Christian. Make a point to speak to this person. Talk with God about growing closer to this potential friend.]

What's Next?

Why are truth and trust so crucial to friendship? Why do we find it so hard to live and give them?

▼

SIX

Build Trust and Live Truth

SESSION OVERVIEW

Purpose:
This session focuses on trust and being yourself, two qualities most people want in a friendship, but few people find easy to give.

Needs:
Adolescents want friends they can trust to treasure their ideas, help them achieve their dreams, and cherish them as they are. At the same time, they find it difficult to give these gifts to others. They don't realize that their encouragement has the power to free their friends to achieve dreams. This session equips group members to give the treasuring, truth, and trust they want. It also encourages them to share who they really are and what they really enjoy. As they do this, they can more deeply enjoy life with friends.

Adolescents fear sharing their deepest thoughts and dreams because someone may think them silly or trample their ideas. They desperately want someone to understand and cherish their interests, ideas, and goals, but don't know how to begin sharing them. So their interaction remains trivial, and each person remains lonely. "You wouldn't like going to that concert would you?" asks one adolescent, hoping the other just might like concerts too. "No, there's a game that night," answers the other, fearing he might think her silly for preferring concerts over ball games. But imagine a response like this: "I've been looking forward to the concert. Would you like to go too?" It's a riskier statement, but it more effectively invites an honest response and can lead to a possible friendship. Because opening themselves to true relationships involves risk, adolescents must discern when to take that risk. Not everyone will cherish, trust, and be true.

In a sense we've come full circle in this study. It may seem we should have started with being yourself and building trust. But it takes time to build the skills of lasting friendships. Because they have had six weeks together, your group members can better give each other the courage to be themselves. As they let God love through them, they become God's instruments of love and friendship. They find ways to free each other to be their best while gently prodding each other to grow. This lesson will sum up the important lessons on friendship we've learned.

Goals:

The goals for the *leader* include
(1) guiding group members to recognize their need for and ability to give treasuring, truth, and trust in friendship;
(2) guiding group members to practice treasuring and trust-building;
(3) reviewing the study to encourage friendship-deepening decisions.

The goals for the *group members* are that they will
(1) picture treasuring, truth, and trust in friendship;
(2) illustrate specific ways to treasure and build trust;
(3) review the unit to make three friendship-changing decisions.

Life Response:

Group members will free their friends to live and love by treasuring them, living the truth, and building trust.

Resource Materials:

____ **Bibles**

____ **pens or pencils**

____ **one copy of *I Thought You Were My Friend!* for each member**

♥ HEARTBEAT

As group members enter, guide them to privately answer these questions and then share them in cell groups of two or three.

Notice Friends You Can Trust

What first attracts you to a friend?

- ☐ sense of humor
- ☐ easy to talk to
- ☐ sincerity
- ☐ values the important things in life
- ☐ expresses faith in God
- ☐ takes life seriously, but not sadly
- ☐ knows how to both work and enjoy
- ☐ understands my goals
- ☐ can talk about God together
- ☐ __________________

- ☐ notice that I can trust this person
- ☐ mutual interests
- ☐ understanding
- ☐ good reputation
- ☐ kindness
- ☐ tells the truth
- ☐ lives the truth
- ☐ shares my goals
- ☐ likes self
- ☐ popular
- ☐ treats all people with kindness
- ☐ __________________

What items from the above list are still important to you as you grow closer to a friend?

What turns you off about:
- ☐ a friend who acts like a parrot—repeating what you said to others:

- ☐ a friend who acts like a chameleon—changing to match the surroundings:

- ☐ a friend who acts like a skunk—spraying everyone in the vicinity when threatened by you or another:

- ☐ a friend who acts like some cats—speaking when in the mood and ignoring you the rest of the time:

- ☐ a friend who acts like a ____________:

Confess a time you have acted like one of these friendship varmints:

Not all idiosyncrasies cause harm. Many can be very helpful. What do you like about:

- ☐ a friend who rejoices like a puppy—jumping and celebrating with you when something good happens:

- ☐ a friend who cares like a grooming chimp—finding the bugs of meanness and selfishness in your life and helping you discard them:

- ☐ a friend who prompts you like a mother bird—nudging you out of your comfort nest to try and succeed at new things:

- ☐ a friend who lets God transform her life like a caterpillar that emerges as a butterfly—motivating you to live a Christlike life by both example and word:

☐ a friend who _______________________________ :

Using the above for samples, draw a combination animal that has characteristics you could trust in a friend. Your friend might make you feel safe like a teddy bear, help you do right no matter how many go the other way like a salmon, and help you fly with joy like an eagle. Use at least three different animal parts in your description. Then label them:

☞ **[HINT: Some of your group members will draw the truth more clearly than they describe. Others may feel hesitant to draw. Assure them that the content of the drawings is central, not the quality of the art they're producing.]**

Notice what matters in friendship to see what kind of friends to pick and what kind of friend to be. If you trust a friend who understands, you won't spend much time with one who ridicules your ideas. This seems obvious, but how many people put up with rude treatment from friends? You hurt God's creation when you put up with rudeness. Instead, seek and build these three crucial friendship qualities:
TREASURING
TRUST
TRUTH (tell the truth and be the true you)

 **LIFELINE**

Treasure Every Person
One of the best ways to bring out trust and truth in friends is to treasure or value them. Complete this phrase from Ephesians 2:10 using your Bible:
For we are God's _______________ created in Christ Jesus to _______________ works, which God prepared in advance for _______ to do.

☞ **[HELP: The words from the NIV are *workmanship, do good, us.* Encourage others to read different translations.]**

We can treasure friends because they are God's workmanship. As we treasure them, we *do the good* God has prepared for *us.* To learn how to treasure, think about how God treasures you. God considers you precious because He made you, similar to the way you treasure something you make. He treasures you by meeting your needs for people, purpose, and skills. He treasures you by providing gifts like nature, love, attention, and security.

Name something you treasure, such as an heirloom or something you've made or worked on. What do you do to show you cherish this item?

How might the same or similar actions show you treasure a specific friend?

Name a need your friend has for people, purpose, skills, love, attention, or security. How could you meet this need?

Together with your group, name at least four other ways to treasure friends.

1.   2.

3.   4.

☞ **[HELP: To treasure a friend means to show you value him or her, to show that person's importance to you. A group member might compare treasuring his car to treasuring a friend by saying "My car needs gasoline and regular tune-ups. Similarly, my friend needs words of encouragement from me to keep him running, and we need to talk regularly to keep our understanding tuned-up." A group member might meet a friend's** needs for people by calling regularly or inviting that friend to her house. Sample additional actions include: Remember what you talked about last time and ask about it; Say things like, "That's a neat idea," "You handled that well," "I like you," "I missed you"; listen without interrupting; compliment an aspect of your friend's character, such as his optimistic outlook or her easygoing personality; spend time together; say you want him at the event; call to check when she is missing from school or church; give a hug; give spontaneous gifts that are meaningful more than expensive; Say "I really like doing (activity) with you" or "you are so good at (activity)"; talk to no matter who is around; let your friends establish relationships with others but take time to keep up with each other; remember a birthday; tell a friend about the complimentary remarks others have made about her.]

☞ [HINT: Make a long treasuring list by forming a circle to include everyone in the group. Each person names a treasuring action he or she can share with another friend. If that person can't name a new way to treasure, he or she must stand until the next turn.]

Treasuring is not always easy, and some friends are more obvious treasures than others. But there are ways to see and bring out the good in even the most prickly of friends. For example, if you stroke a porcupine in the right direction, she feels soft and acts kindly. How have you seen treasuring bring out the good in a person?

Reread Ephesians 2:10. Who might God want you to treasure right now? How?

Build Trust with Those Who Treasure You

Once you feel valued, you can build trust. Read Proverbs 15:1-4 for four actions that build trust. Below each statement draw a cartoon that illustrates each trust action by showing a way to do it or by showing a catastrophe that results when you don't do it:

Trust Action A: *A* ________ *answer turns away* ________ . The opposite of this is to speak harshly and cause anger.

Trust Action B: *The tongue of the* ________ *commends* ________ . This means to say what is helpful and useful to people. It also means to know truth when you see it. The opposite is to say foolish or stupid words.

Trust Action C: *The* ________ *of the Lord are* ________ *keeping watch on the* ________ *and the* ________. I am motivated to take good care of friends and be real with them because God is watching.

Trust Action D: *The tongue that brings* ________ *is a tree of* ________, *but a* ________ *tongue* ________ *the spirit.* Lying or being other than myself doesn't make me look good—it hurts my friends.

☞ **[HELP: A—gentle, wrath; B—wise, knowledge; C—eyes, everywhere, wicked, good; D—healing, life, deceitful, crushes.]**

Talk with God about helping you do all four trust-building actions. Write the name and situation He gives you for living each:

Proverbs 15:1:

Proverbs 15:2:

Proverbs 15:3:

Proverbs 15:4:

IMPORTANT: Trust is not blind. It is not letting your friend do as he wants without evaluation or checking. It is believing the best about a person and helping him achieve it. This includes giving the boundaries that keep him from wrongdoing.

Be Your True Self

You build trust when you care for your friend who tells you his ideas and dreams. You also build trust when you have courage to tell your friend what you dream and think. We call this being ourselves. Read the following truth-revealing activities and circle the number that most closely matches how you usually respond, with 1 as "nearly impossible" and 10 as "comes easily."

Tell a private thought

1   2   3   4   5   6   7   8   9   10

Talk about an idea

1   2   3   4   5   6   7   8   9   10

Describe a dream

1   2   3   4   5   6   7   8   9   10

Give a compliment

1   2   3   4   5   6   7   8   9   10

Say hello to someone new

1   2   3   4   5   6   7   8   9   10

Express what I really like to do instead of
going to a ball game or the mall

1 2 3 4 5 6 7 8 9 10

Confide in someone about a worry

1 2 3 4 5 6 7 8 9 10

Say what I really think and believe rather than
what I think my friend wants me to say

1 2 3 4 5 6 7 8 9 10

Not everyone will cherish and be true when you trust them. But many people are waiting to know the real you. How can you tell the difference?

Invite God to help you discern who to share with and what to share. As you pray, write next to each action on the survey above a way you will do it and a person with whom you will do it.

☞ **[HINT: Suggest that group members pray for one another's ability to trust. This includes not only sharing themselves but perceiving who will receive that sharing in a caring manner. Do not force group members to tell the specific areas, but welcome voluntary reporting as a way to discover that others struggle too.]**

Live the Truth

Trust, treasuring, and honest sharing blend to form friendship loyalty. What phrase does Proverbs 18:24 use to describe loyalty?

☞ **[HELP: Stick closer than a brother.]**

The very qualities that make loyalty strong—trust and devotion—can be abused. True loyalty must be based in truth and love. How do the situations below contrast with the loyalty friends should show to each other?

1. You suspect that your friend Wes may be involved with a group that has been spray-painting graffiti on school property. One night Wes comes over to visit you. He has splotches of bright green paint on his hands and on the sweatshirt he's wearing. When you ask him what he has been doing, Wes eventually admits that he was spray-painting the goalposts and bleachers around the football field. He begs you not to say anything because it could jeopardize his chances of winning a scholarship. Besides, he says, nobody is getting hurt. He hints around that he might cause trouble for you if you decide to tell anyone.

2. Marla tells you her woeful story that her mom has grounded her from dating for a month. When you volunteer to have her over to take her mind off it, she says "That would be great! Now I can go out with Patrick and my mom will never know!" You say that's not what you had in mind. You're sorry about her not getting to see Patrick, but you can't deceive her mom. Marla storms, "I thought you were my friend!"

3. J. J. treats you rotten, sometimes calling, sometimes not, sometimes paying attention to you and other times ignoring you. You attribute this to his fickle nature but decide to make other friends too. J. J. hits the roof when he finds out about your decision. He snarls, "I thought you cared! Some loyal friend you are running around with other people!" You feel that since J. J. has not shown you loyalty, you are not being disloyal for spending time with others. There's room for more than one friend, and you need people who will be consistent.

☞ **[HELP: Help group members discover that loyalty is not doing whatever your friend asks, but consistently acting in ways that show care. Loyalty includes doing right, treating people right, believing the right ideas. Explain that loyalty becomes destructive when it ex-**

cuses wrong, such as covering up for a friend's crime. It also becomes destructive when it does not help a friend stop a cruel habit like laughing at people. Explain that loyalty does not mean putting up with wrong behavior. Loyalty prompts a friend to change. To explore this further, ask: What's the difference between loyalty and compromising the truth to please a friend? Between loyalty and letting yourself be used? Between loyalty and tolerance of questionable behavior? Between loyalty and putting your friend before God? Encourage the group to choose actions because they're right, not because a friend asks you to do them.]

Choose the Good

Treasuring, trust, and loyalty make it easier for you to be the true you. Which of your many roles is the true you? The best one. We all have potential for incredible good or disastrous evil. It's the choice we have as free human beings created by God. So choose to express the good, depending on God for guidance.

Name a friend who brings out the good in you: ________________. With what actions does this friend do this for you?

How have you brought out the good in a friend?

 **BODYLIFE**

Build Treasuring, Trust-building, and True Friendships
Being yourself and living the truth are foundational to the friendship skills in every chapter of this book. You can be a treasuring, trust-building, true friend. Find ways God wants you to do this by looking through the six sessions we've shared. For each number, write the theme of that chapter and explain how the ideas have impacted your life:

1.

2.

3.

4.

5.

6.

Life Response

You can grow solid friendships. Do this word by word and action by action. Begin with three actions from this list. Choose the ones you think God, your friendship Designer, wants you to do first:

- [ ] **A**.ttention paid to my friendships so I can give greater happiness.
- [ ] **B**.e there for my friend during a rough time.
- [ ] **C**.laim responsibility for making my friendships honest and real.
- [ ] **D**.iscover what God has to say about friendships.
- [ ] **E**.xit an unhealthy friendship.
- [ ] **F**.riends know they can count on me.
- [ ] **G**.row more confident in talking to people.
- [ ] **H**.ide self-centeredness so I can better see and meet another's need.
- [ ] **I**.nterest shown in someone I haven't shown interest in before.
- [ ] **J**.okes that put people down must stop.
- [ ] **K**.eep in step with the Spirit.
- [ ] **L**.isten more attentively to _______.
- [ ] **M**.yths of friendship should be corrected.
- [ ] **N**.otice that my friend needs _______ and provide it by . . .
- [ ] **O**.penly solve problems rather than use grudges, gossip, or getting back.

☐ **P**.eople matter more than position or status.
☐ **Q**.uit worrying about what people think of me and focus on thinking well of them.
☐ **R**.epair a broken friendship.
☐ **S**.ay what I mean so people can trust my words.
☐ **T**.ear down my reluctance to be honest.
☐ **U**.ntruths and insincerity banned from my life.
☐ **V**.iew people the way God does, valuing joy, honesty, kindness, and other qualities.
☐ **W**.atch that my actions match God's ways.
☐ **X**.amine my friends' motives and choose the ones who obey God.
☐ **Y**.es to opening my circle to include more people.
☐ **Z**.eal for helping my friend be her best.

☞ **[HINT: Prompt group members to spell a word with the first letters of the actions they choose and to use their name as they report. Lynn might say: "To grow H.A.T. friendships, I, Lynn, will—*H*ide self-centeredness to better see and meet another's need; pay *A*ttention to my friends no matter who's around; *T*ear down walls that prevent me from being honest."]**

☞ **[HELP: Additional Life Responses to include if time allows or to suggest for home follow-through:**

1. Keep a journal about how your friends treat you and how you treat them. Read your entries monthly and make one change for the better in your friendships. Find ways to let your friendships bring good for God.

2. Thank God daily for the way He made you. How can He use your personality to bring good to people and to this world?

Care for your friends as God cares for you, and choose friends who love you as God loves you.

I Thought You Were My Friend!

Please take a minute to fill out and mail this form giving us your candid reaction to this material. Thanks for your help!

In what setting did you use this Small Group Study? (Sunday School, youth group, midweek Bible study, etc.) _____________

How many young people were in your group? _____________

What was the age range of those in your group? _____________

How long was your average meeting? _____________

Do you plan to use other SonPower Small Group Studies? _____ Why or why not?

Did you and your young people enjoy this study? Why or why not?

What are the strengths and/or weaknesses of this leader's edition?

What are the strengths and/or weaknesses of the student book?

Would you like more information on SonPower Youth Sources?

Name	_____________________
Church name	_____________________
Church address	_____________________
	_____________________
Church phone	(______)_____________
Church size	_____________________

SGY07

SonPower Youth Sources Editor
Victor Books
1825 College Avenue
Wheaton, Illinois 60187